Handy Maryland Genealogy Handbook

I0450653

By Gary L. Morris

©2015 Gary L. Morris

ISBN-13: 978-1507721551

ISBN-10: 1507721552

Table of Contents

Notes

Genealogical Research in Maryland

Tracing your family history in Maryland can be a fascinating trip through time. Maryland was one of the original thirteen colonies, and as such there is a wealth of genealogical records to be found for the state. Tracking these records down can be an ominous task, but don't worry, we know just where they are, and we'll show you which records you'll need, and help you to understand:

1. What they are
2. Where to find them
3. How to use them

These records can be found both online and off, so we'll introduce you to online websites, indexes and databases, as well as brick-and-mortar repositories and other institutions that will help with your research in Maryland. So that you will have a more comprehensive understanding of these records, we have provided a brief history of the "Old Line State" to illustrate what type of records may have been generated during specific time periods. That information will assist you in pinpointing times and locations on which to focus the search for your Maryland ancestors and their records.

A Brief History of Maryland

The Paleo-Indians first inhabited Maryland nearly 10,000 years ago. By the year 1,000 B.C., nearly 8,000 Native Americans comprising approximately 40 tribes lived in the area. The first European to visit the area was the Italian explorer Giovanni da Verrazano who visited the Chesapeake Bay, which Captain John Smith called it a place perfect for man's habitation. The first trading post was set up on Kent Island in 1631 by the fur trader William Claiborne, and the first official settlement was founded at St. Mary's City in 1634.

Maryland began as a colony in 1632 when George Calvert, was given permission by Britain's King Charles I to start a colony in the Chesapeake area. The following year the British ships the *Dove* and the *Ark* carrying settlers who founded St. Mary's City. In 1649, Puritans fleeing religious prosecution from Great Britain founded Providence. In spite of the highly religious nature of the majority of Maryland residents, slavery was made legal in 1664, binding slaves to their owners for life.

In 1729, as Maryland began to swiftly develop its manufacturing sector, Baltimore was founded to expedite the export of goods. A series of ironworks sprung up, and Maryland also became a major exporter of tobacco and producer of flour. The Native Americans of Maryland were not as organized as tribes elsewhere, and put up little resistance to the European efforts to grab their land. Finally in 1744, the colony purchased the remainder of Native American land holdings of what would become the colony of Maryland.

Resistance to the British taxes began to take hold in the colony during the 1760's and a Maryland chapter of the Sons of Liberty was organized. Maryland signed the Bush Declaration which called for independence from Great Britain in 1775, and when war broke out in 1776, sent its troops to join the forces of George Washington. Maryland soldiers fought in many of the major battles and contributed greatly to the American victory.

From 1783 until August of 1784, the city of Annapolis was the capital of the new America. It was there that the Treaty of Paris was signed, ending the Revolutionary War. When Maryland ratified the Constitution on April 28, 1788, it became the seventh state.

As a slave state, Maryland joined the union cause when Civil War broke out, and it was in the state that the first blood shed in the conflict took place during the Baltimore Riot in 1861. Several thousand citizens of Maryland fled to Virginia to fight for the Confederacy after the Baltimore Riot, and many who remained during and after the war continued to support slavery. Many Marylanders opposed the abolition of slavery until the state's new constitution finally ended the practice when it was passed on October 13, 1864, though by a narrow margin of 30,174 to 29,799.

Important Dates in Maryland History

1608 - Captain John Smith explores the Chesapeake Bay

1631 - English trading post established on Kent Island

1632 - Maryland Charter granted to Cecilius Calvert by King Charles I

1633 - 1634 - Ark and Dove arrive at St. Clements Island; St. Mary's City founded

1664 - Slavery allowed by law in Maryland

1695 - Annapolis becomes the capital of Maryland

1729 - Baltimore founded

1783 - Annapolis became the nation's capital from November 1783 until August

1784 - Congress ratifies the Treaty of Paris in Annapolis

1788 - Maryland becomes the seventh state

1813 - British raid Havre de Grace during the War of 1812

1861 - First bloodshed of Civil War occurs in Baltimore

1862 - Confederate forces defeated at Antietam

1864 - Maryland abolishes slavery

1867 - Present Maryland Constitution adopted

Famous Battles Fought in Maryland

In addition to the first bloodshed of the Civil War being shed in Maryland during the **Baltimore Riot of 1861;** the bloodiest and one of the most famous battles of the conflict, the **Battle of Antietam** also took place on Maryland soil. Two other major battles, the **Battle of Front Royal**, and the **Battle of Monocacy** were also fought in Maryland. The War of 1812 saw the **British Attack on Fort McHenry** take place in Baltimore. This event inspired Francis Scott Key to compose the "Star Spangled Banner", America's long standing national anthem.

These battle accounts that do exist can be very effective in uncovering the military records of your ancestor. They can tell you what regiments fought in which battles, and often include the names and ranks of many officers and enlisted men.

Baltimore Riot of 1861: http://www.historynet.com/baltimore-riot-of-1861.htm

Battle of Antietam:
http://www.civilwar.org/battlefields/antietam.html

Battle of Front Royal:
http://www.nps.gov/history/hps/abpp/shenandoah/svs3-3.html

Battle of Monocacy:
http://www.civilwar.org/battlefields/monocacy.html

British Attack on Fort McHenry:
http://www.eighteentwelve.ca/?q=eng/Topic/57

Common Maryland Genealogical Issues and Resources to Overcome Them

Boundary Changes: Boundary changes are a common obstacle when researching Maryland ancestors. You could be searching for an ancestor's record in one county when in fact it is stored in a different one due to historical county boundary changes.

The **Atlas of Historical County Boundaries** can help you to overcome that problem. It provides a chronological listing of every boundary change that has occurred in the history of Maryland.

Atlas of Historical County Boundaries: http://publications.newberry.org/ahcbp/documents/MD_Consolidate d_Chronology.htm#Consolidated_Chronology

Name Changes: Surname changes, variations, and misspellings can complicate genealogical research. It is important to check all spelling variations. Soundex, a program that indexes names by sound, is a useful first step, but you can't rely on it completely as some name variations result in different Soundex codes. The surnames could be different, but the first name may be different too. You can also find records filed under initials, middle names, and nicknames as well, so you will need to **get creative with surname variations** and spellings in order to cover all the possibilities. For help with surname variations read our instructional article on **How to Use Soundex.**

get creative with surname variations: http://obituarieshelp.org/blog/?p=634

How to Use Soundex: http://obituarieshelp.org/blog/?p=505

Maryland Genealogical Organizations and Archives

Genealogical resources include not only records, but the organizations that house them, or can direct you to them. These institutions include: *Archives, Libraries, Genealogical Societies, Family History Centers, Universities, Churches, and Museums.*

Following are links to their websites, their physical addresses, and a summary of the records you can find there.

Archives and Libraries

Maryland State Archives - county records, marriage licenses, land records, naturalization dockets, slave records, wills, military records, death records, birth records, baptisms, census records, and more

350 Rowe Boulevard
Annapolis, MD 21401
Tel: toll free: (800) 235-4045 or (410) 260-6400

Maryland State Archives:
http://msa.maryland.gov/msa/homepage/html/family.html

National Archives at Philadelphia – historically significant records of the Federal Agencies and Courts, in Delaware, Maryland, Pennsylvania, Virginia, and West Virginia, dating from 1789 to the present including: naturalization records, census records, military records, and ships passenger lists

380 Trapelo Road
Waltham, MA 02154
Telephone: 617-647-8100
Fax: 617-647-8460

National Archives at Philadelphia:
http://www.archives.gov/philadelphia/public/family-history.html#records

Maryland State Law Library - maps, newspapers, the federal censuses and 1850 mortality schedules

Robert C. Murphy Courts of Appeal Building
361 Rowe Blvd.
Annapolis, MD 21401
Phone: 410.260.1430
Fax 410.260.1572

Maryland State Law Library:
http://www.lawlib.state.md.us/researchtools/databases.html

Baltimore City Archives - municipal records (1756–1938), indexes to Port of Baltimore ships' passenger lists (1833–66), index to naturalizations in the U.S. circuit and district courts for Maryland (1797–1951), maps, tax records from 1798, and voter registrations (1838, 1839, 1868, and 1877–89)

2615 Mathews St
Baltimore MD 21218
Tel: 410-396-3884
Email: baltimorecityarchives@gmail.com

Baltimore City Archives: http://baltimorecityhistory.net/

Maryland Genealogical and Historical Societies

Genealogical and historical societies have access to extensive catalogues of genealogical data. They are also able to offer expert guidance for genealogical researchers. Many members are professional genealogists who are most willing to share their expertise in finding ancestors.

Maryland Genealogical Society – historical newspapers, manuscripts, cemetery records, church records

Maryland Genealogical Society
201 West Monument Street
Baltimore, MD 21201
Email: info@mdgensoc.org

Maryland Genealogical Society: http://www.mdgensoc.org/

Maryland Historical Society – manuscripts, historical maps and photographs, oral histories, journals and magazines

201 W. Monument St.
Baltimore, MD 21201-4674
Tel: 410-685-3750

Maryland Historical Society:
http://www.mdhs.org/library/collections-overview

Baltimore County Genealogical Society – surnames list, genealogical indexes, various books and other resources

P.O. Box 10085
Towson, MD 21285-0085

Email: info@baltimoregenealogysociety.org

Baltimore County Genealogical Society:
http://www.baltimoregenealogysociety.org/

Maryland Mailing Lists

Mailing lists are internet based facilities that use email to distribute a single message to all who subscribe to it. When information on a particular surname, new records, or any other important genealogy information related to the mailing list topic becomes available, the subscribers are alerted to it. Joining a mailing list is an excellent way to stay up to date on Maryland genealogy research topics. Rootsweb have an extensive listing of **Maryland Mailing Lists** on a variety of topics.

Maryland Mailing Lists:
http://lists.rootsweb.ancestry.com/index/usa/MD/misc.html

Maryland Message Boards

A message board is another internet based facility where people can post questions about a specific genealogy topic and have it answered by other genealogists. If you have questions about a surname, record type, or research topic, you can post your question and other researchers and genealogists will help you with the answer. Be sure to check back regularly, as the answers are not emailed to you. The Maryland Message Boards at **Rootsweb** are completely free to use.

Rootsweb:
http://boards.rootsweb.com/localities.northam.usa.states/mb.ashx

<u>Maryland Newspapers and Periodicals</u>

Many genealogy periodicals and historical newspapers contain reprinted copies of family genealogies, transcripts of family Bible records, information about local records and archives, census indexes, church records, queries, land records, obituaries, court records, cemetery records, and wills. The following sites have historical Maryland newspapers and periodicals that you can search online or on-site.

Maryland Newspaper Project – Baltimore Sun, 1837-1985, and 1990 to present, Afro-American, 1893-1988

Maryland Newspaper Project: http://speccol.mdarchives.state.md.us/pages/newspaper/index.aspx

Maryland Historical Society – approximately 220 journals, magazines, and newsletters, mostly relating to history and genealogy

201 W. Monument St.
Baltimore, MD 21201-4674
Tel: 410-685-3750

Maryland Historical Society: http://www.mdhs.org/library/family-and-local-history-journals-and-magazines

GenealogyBank.com – free searchable database of Maryland newspaper archives, 1728–1922

GenealogyBank.com: http://www.genealogybank.com/gbnk/newspapers/explore/USA/Maryland/

Library of Congress Digital Newspaper Directory – free searchable database of historical U.S. newspapers dating from 1690-present

Library of Congress Digital Newspaper Directory: http://chroniclingamerica.loc.gov/search/titles/

The Online Books Page – links to historical Maryland books and periodicals available for viewing online, dating from mid-16th century

The Online Books Page: http://onlinebooks.library.upenn.edu

NewspaperArchive.com – largest online database of historical newspapers in the world.

NewspaperArchive.com: http://newspaperarchive.com/

Historical Maryland Maps and Gazetteers

Maps are an integral part of genealogical research. They help us to locate landmarks, towns, cities, parishes, states, provinces, waterways and roads and streets. They also help us to determine when and where boundary changes might have taken place, and give us a visualization of the area we're researching in.

For locating place names, a gazetteer is the best possible resource for any genealogist. Gazetteers are also sometimes called "place name dictionaries", and can help you to locate the area in which you need to conduct research. Below are links to the maps and gazetteers for research in Maryland.

Peabody GNIS Service – Maryland:
http://peabody.research.yale.edu/cgi-bin/Query.GNIS?ST=Maryland&SU=1

Color Landform Atlas – Maryland:
http://fermi.jhuapl.edu/states/md_0.html

1985 U.S. Atlas: http://www.livgenmi.com/1895/MD/

Maryland Hometown Locator:
http://maryland.hometownlocator.com/

Maryland City Directories
.

City directories are similar to telephone directories in that they list the residents of a particular area. The difference though is what is important to genealogists, and that is they pre-date telephone directories. You can find an ancestor's information such as their street address, place of employment, occupation, or the name of their spouse. A one-stop-shop for finding city directories in Maryland is the **Maryland Online Historical Directories** which contains a listing of every available online historical directory related to Maryland.

Maryland Online Historical Directories:
https://sites.google.com/site/onlinedirectorysite/Home/usa/md

Baltimore City Archives - a comprehensive list of Maryland City Directories dating from 1752

2615 Mathews St
Baltimore MD 21218
Tel: 410-396-3884

Baltimore City Archives: http://baltimorecityhistory.net/baltimore-city-directories/

Maryland Genealogical Records

Birth, Death, Marriage and Divorce Records – Also known as vital records, birth, death, and marriage certificates are the most basic, yet most important records attached to your ancestor. The reason for their importance is that they not only place your ancestor in a specific place at a definite time, but potentially connect the individual to other relatives. Below is a list of repositories and websites where you can find Maryland vital records.

Maryland Division of Vital Records – birth, death, marriage, and divorce records from mid-twentieth century and some older records

6550 Reisterstown Road
Reisterstown Road Plaza
Baltimore, MD 21215
Tel: (410) 764-3038

Maryland Division of Vital Records:
http://dhmh.maryland.gov/vsa/SitePages/Home.aspx

Maryland State Archives - older death, birth, and marriages dating from 19th century records, and more

350 Rowe Boulevard
Annapolis, MD 21401
Tel: toll free: (800) 235-4045 or (410) 260-6400

Maryland State Archives:
http://guide.mdsa.net/state.cfm?qualifier=SM

A searchable online index is the **Maryland State Archives Death Index** – Death index for the twenty-three counties other than Baltimore City for 1898-1944, and for Baltimore City from 1875 to 1972

Maryland State Archives Death Index:
http://www.mdvitalrec.net/cfm/index.cfm

Family Search also has the following indexes that can be searched for free online:

Maryland Births and Christenings, 1650-1995:
https://familysearch.org/search/collection/1674912

Maryland Deaths and Burials, 1877-1992:
https://familysearch.org/search/collection/1675198

Maryland Marriages, 1666-1970:
https://familysearch.org/search/collection/1675199

Census Reports

Census records are among the most important genealogical documents for placing your ancestor in a particular place at a specific time. Like BDM records, they can also lead you to other ancestors, particularly those who were living under the authority of the head of household.

Federal census records for Maryland exist from 1790–1930 and can be found at:

National Archives at Philadelphia – federal census records, 1790-1930

380 Trapelo Road
Waltham, MA 02154
Telephone: 617-647-8100
Fax: 617-647-8460

National Archives at Philadelphia:
http://www.archives.gov/philadelphia/public/family-history.html#records

Maryland State Archives – census records 1790-1920, district enumerations, 1720-1850

350 Rowe Boulevard
Annapolis, MD 21401
Tel: toll free: (800) 235-4045 or (410) 260-6400

Maryland State Archives:
http://guide.mdsa.net/state.cfm?qualifier=SM

The **Free Census Project** has transcribed many Maryland indexes and new material is added daily

Free Census Project: http://usgwcensus.org/cenfiles/md.htm

Access Genealogy – Maryland county census records from 1790

Access Genealogy:
http://www.accessgenealogy.com/census/Maryland-census-records.htm

African American Census Schedules Online – slave schedules, mortality schedules, slave-owners census

African American Census Schedules Online:
http://www.afrigeneas.com/aacensus/ga/

Native Americans in Census Records (US National Archives)

Native Americans in Census Records:
http://www.archives.gov/research/census/native-americans/

Maryland Church Records

Church and synagogue records are a valuable resource, especially for baptisms, marriages, and burials that took place before 1900. You will need to at least have an idea of your ancestor's religious denomination, and in most cases you will have to visit a brick and mortar establishment to view them.

Most church records are kept by the individual church, although in some denominations, records are placed in a regional archive or maintained at the diocesan level. Local Historical Societies are sometimes the repository for the state's older church records. Below are links archives that maintain church records, as well as a few databases that can be viewed online.

The **Family History Library** contains many church records from a variety of denominations on microfilm.

Family History Library:
http://familysearch.org/learn/wiki/en/Family_History_Library

Maryland Genealogical Society – church records from First German United Evangelical Church (Baltimore City, Maryland), Saint Mary's Govans Catholic Church (Baltimore City, Maryland), and Saint Paul's Fifth German Reformed Church (Baltimore City, Maryland) from 1850-1919

Maryland Genealogical Society
201 West Monument Street
Baltimore, MD 21201
Email: info@mdgensoc.org

Maryland Genealogical Society: http://www.mdgensoc.org/

Maryland State Archives – Episcopalian parish records from the Protestant Episcopal Diocese of Washington, Diocese of Easton, Diocese of Maryland, parish records for most of the state, Catholic records from the Catholic Archdiocese of Baltimore, Quaker records

350 Rowe Boulevard
Annapolis, MD 21401
Tel: toll free: (800) 235-4045 or (410) 260-6400

Maryland State Archives :
http://guide.mdsa.net/state.cfm?qualifier=SM

Central Repositories for Denominational Records

Most of the records of individual denominations are kept in central repositories. Below is a list of the major congregational archives for Maryland with links to their websites, physical addresses, and contact information.

Baptist

Baptist Convention of Maryland/Delaware
10255 Old Columbia
Columbia, MD 21046
Telephone: 800-466-5290 + 0 or 410-667-9169
Fax: 410-290-7040

Baptist Convention of Maryland/Delaware: http://bcmd.org/

United Baptist Missionary Convention – African American records

940 Madison Avenue
Baltimore, MD 21201
Telephone: 410-523-2950
Fax: 410-523-0250

United Baptist Missionary Convention: http://ubmcofmd.org/

Episcopalian

Archives of the Episcopal Church
P.O. Box 2247
Austin, TX 78768
Telephone: 512-472-6816
Fax: 512-480-0437
E-mail: Research@episcopalarchives.org

Archives of the Episcopal Church:
http://www.episcopalarchives.org/

Church of Jesus Christ of Latter-day Saints (Mormons)

Early Mormon Church records for Maryland can be found on film located at the LDS Family History Library in Salt Lake City and can be searched via the **Family History Library Catalog**

Family History Library Catalog:
https://familysearch.org/eng/Library/FHLC/frameset_fhlc.asp

Lutheran

Archives of the Delaware-Maryland Synod
Evangelical Lutheran Church in America
700 Light St.
Towson, MD 21204-7570
Telephone: 410-825-9520
Fax: 410-825-6745

Archives of the Delaware-Maryland Synod:
http://www.elca.org/Who-We-Are/History/ELCA-Archives.aspx

Methodist

United Methodist Historical Society
Lovely Lane Museum Library
2200 St. Paul Street
Baltimore, MD 21218-5897
Telephone: 410-889-4458
Fax: 410-889-1501

United Methodist Historical Society:
http://www.lovelylanemuseum.org/

Presbyterian

Presbyterian Historical Society
425 Lombard Street Philadelphia, PA 19147-1516
Telephone: 215-627-1852
Fax: 215-627-0509
Email: refdesk@history.pcusa.org

Presbyterian Historical Society: http://www.history.pcusa.org/

Roman Catholic

Archives of Archdiocese of Baltimore
5400 Roland Avenue
Baltimore, MD 22120
Telephone: 410-864-4074
Fax: 410-864-3690
Email: archives@stmarys.edu

Archives of Archdiocese of Baltimore:
http://www.stmarys.edu/archives/arc_coll_ab.htm

Maryland Military Records

More than 40 million Americans have participated in some time of war service since America was colonized. The chance of finding your ancestor amongst those records is exceptionally high. Military records can even reveal individuals who never actually served, such as those who registered for the two World Wars but were never called to duty.

Below are a number of links to websites and archives that contain Maryland military records.

Maryland State Archives – Adjutant Generals records, militia appointments, enrollments, muster rolls, Commissioner of Army Accounts records (pay accounts, letter books), pension rolls, bounty rolls,

350 Rowe Boulevard
Annapolis, MD 21401
Tel: toll free: (800) 235-4045 or (410) 260-6400

Maryland State Archives:
http://guide.mdsa.net/state.cfm?qualifier=SM

National Archives at Philadelphia – Revolutionary War veteran's pension and bounty land warrants, World War I Draft Registration Cards, World War II Fourth Enumeration Draft Registration Cards

380 Trapelo Road
Waltham, MA 02154
Telephone: 617-647-8100
Fax: 617-647-8460

National Archives at Philadelphia:
http://www.archives.gov/philadelphia/public/family-history.html#records

U.S. National Archives – WWI Draft registration cards, casualties lists, WWI and WWII service records, Korean War records, Vietnam War records, Civil War and Spanish-American War records, and casualties lists.

U.S. National Archives:
http://www.archives.gov/research/military/veterans/online.html

US Department of Veterans Affairs Nationwide Gravesite Locator – includes information on veterans and their family members buried in veterans and military cemeteries having a government grave marker.

US Department of Veterans Affairs Nationwide Gravesite Locator: http://gravelocator.cem.va.gov/

You may also find your ancestor's military records in the following databases:

Maryland Civil War Service Records of Confederate Soldiers, 1861-1865: https://familysearch.org/search/collection/1932373

Maryland Civil War Service Records of Union Soldiers, 1861-1865: https://familysearch.org/search/collection/1932407

United States General Index to Pension Files, 1861-1934: https://familysearch.org/search/collection/1919699

United States Index to Service Records, War with Spain, 1898: https://familysearch.org/search/collection/1919583

United States Index to Indian Wars Pension Files, 1892-1926 – military pension records of soldiers who fought in the Indian Wars between 1817 and 1898

United States Index to Indian Wars Pension Files, 1892-1926: https://familysearch.org/search/collection/1979427

United States Registers of Enlistments in the U.S. Army, 1798-1914 - index of men who enlisted in the United States Army, 1798-1914.

United States Registers of Enlistments in the U.S. Army, 1798-1914: https://familysearch.org/search/collection/1880762

United States Mexican War Pension Index, 1887-1926 - index to Mexican War pension files for service between 1846 and 1848

United States Mexican War Pension Index, 1887-1926: https://familysearch.org/search/collection/1979390

Civil War Soldiers Service Records - Service records for both Union and Confederate soldiers indexed by soldier's name, rank, and unit.

Civil War Soldier Service Records: http://go.fold3.com/civilwar_records/

Maryland Cemetery Records

As convenient as it is to search cemetery records online, keep in mind that there are a few disadvantages over visiting a cemetery in person. They are:

- Tombstone information is not always accurately transcribed
- The arrangement of the graves in a cemetery can be crucial as family members are often buried next to each other or in the same grave. This arrangement is not always preserved in the alphabetical indexes that are found online.

With that information in mind, the following websites have databases that can be searched online for Maryland Cemetery records.

Maryland Tombstone Transcription Project - death and burial records

Maryland Tombstone Transcription Project:
http://www.usgwtombstones.org/maryland/maryland.html

African American Cemeteries Online – African American, slave, and Native American cemetery records

African American Cemeteries Online:
http://africanamericancemeteries.com/ar/

Access Genealogy – huge database of Maryland cemetery record transcriptions

Access Genealogy:
http://www.accessgenealogy.com/cemetery/maryland-cemetery-records.htm

Find a Grave – over 100 million grave records can be searched on this site. Search can be conducted by name, location, or cemetery name.

Find a Grave: http://www.findagrave.com/

Interment.net - A free online database containing approximately 4 million cemetery records from around the world.

Interment.net: http://www.interment.net/

Billion Graves – as the name implies, you can search a billion records including headstone photos, transcriptions, cemetery records, and grave locations.

Billion Graves:
http://billiongraves.com/pages/search/index.php#cemetery

Maryland Obituaries

Obituaries can reveal a wealth about our ancestor and other relatives. You can search our **Maryland Newspaper Obituaries Listings** from hundreds of Maryland newspapers online for free.

Maryland Newspaper Obituaries Listings:
http://obituarieshelp.org/maryland_newspaper_obituaries.html

Maryland Wills and Probate Records

The documents found in a probate packet may include a complete inventory of a person's estate, newspaper entries, witness testimony, a copy of a will, list of debtors and creditors, names of executors or trustees, names of heirs. They can not only tell you about the ancestor you're currently researching, but lead to other ancestors.

Probate records in Maryland are under the jurisdiction of the **Register of Wills** where you can even **Search Maryland Estate Records Online.**

Register of Wills link: http://registers.maryland.gov/main/

Search Maryland Estate Records Online: http://registers.maryland.gov/main/search.html

The **Maryland State Archives** has an online index of **Early Colonial Probate Records, 1634-1777** that is free to search online

Early Colonial Probate Records, 1634-1777: http://msa.maryland.gov/megafile/msa/stagsere/se1/se4/000000/html

Family Search has the following indexes that can be searched online for free:

Maryland Probate Estate and Guardianship Files, 1796-1940: https://familysearch.org/search/collection/1542664

Maryland Register of Wills Books, 1629-1999: https://familysearch.org/search/collection/1803986

Maryland Immigration and Naturalization Records

The naturalization process generated many types of records, including petitions, declarations of intention, and oaths of allegiance. These records can provide family historians with information such as a person's birth date and place of birth, immigration year, marital status, spouse information, occupation, witnesses' names and addresses, and more.

The **US National Archives** has a huge collection of Ship's Passenger lists for Maryland and the surrounding east coast ports where immigrants would have arrived.

US National Archives:
http://www.archives.gov/research/immigration/passenger-arrival.html

Maryland State Archives – convicts records, merchants records, Early Settlers List, Naturalizations, Provincial, Index, 1637-1776, Naturalizations, Index, 1777-1917, Naturalizations Index, 1796-1933, Naturalizations, Baltimore Index, 1852-1918, Naturalizations, Federal Index, 1797-1906, 1925-1951 and naturalizations of soldiers, 1918-1923

350 Rowe Boulevard
Annapolis, MD 21401
Tel: toll free: (800) 235-4045 or (410) 260-6400

Maryland State Archives:
http://guide.mdsa.net/viewer.cfm?page=naturalization

Family Search has the following indexes that can be searched online for free:

Maryland, Baltimore Passenger Lists, 1820-1948:
https://familysearch.org/search/collection/2018318

Maryland, Baltimore, Passenger, and Crew Lists of Vessels and Airplanes, 1954-1957:
https://familysearch.org/search/collection/2072742

Maryland, Naturalization Indexes, 1797-1951:
https://familysearch.org/search/collection/1838829

Maryland, Naturalization Petitions, 1906-1931:
https://familysearch.org/search/collection/1854313

Maryland Native American Records

Maryland GenWeb – multiple resources for researching the genealogy of Maryland Native American tribes

Maryland GenWeb:
http://www.rootsweb.ancestry.com/~mdgwnar/

Access Genealogy – Maryland Native American census records, tribal histories, and much more

Access Genealogy:
http://www.accessgenealogy.com/native/maryland-indian-tribes.htm

U.S. National Archives - information on American Indians who maintained their ties to Federally-recognized Tribes (1830-1970).

U.S. National Archives: http://www.archives.gov/research/native-americans/

Records of the Bureau of Indian Affairs (BIA):
http://www.archives.gov/research/guide-fed-records/groups/075.html

American Indians Records Repository - records dating from the 1700s including trust, education and other historic Indian Affairs records

American Indian Records Repository
Meritex Enterprises
17501 West 98th Street
Lenexa, KS 66219
Phone: 913-888-0601

American Indians Records Repository:
http://www.doi.gov/ost/records_mgmt/american-indian-records-repository.cfm

Missing Matriarchs – Resources for Researching Female Maryland Ancestors

Looking for female ancestors requires an adjustment of how we view traditional records sources. A woman's identity was often under that of her husband, and often individual records for them can be difficult to locate. The following resources are effective in locating female ancestors in Maryland where traditional records may not reveal them.

Bibliographies

- *Private Acts in Public Places: A Social History of Divorce in the Formative Era of American Family Law,* Richard H. Chused (University of Pennsylvania Press, 1994)
- *A Maryland Album: Quilting Traditions,* Gloria Seaman Allen (Rutledge Hill Press, 1995)
- *Maryland Women,* Margie H. Luckett (The Author, 1931)
- *A Digest of the Law of Husband and Wife in Maryland,* David Steward and Francis Casey (Baltimore: n.p. 1881)

Selected Resources for Maryland Women's History

National Women's Studies Association
University of Maryland at College Park
College Park, MD 20742

Sojourner Truth Room
Prince George's County Memorial Library
6200 Oxon Hill Rd.
Oxon Hill, MD 20745

Common Maryland Surnames

The following surnames are among the most common in Maryland and are also being currently researched by other genealogists. If you find your surname here, there is a chance that some research has already been performed on your ancestor.

ABE, ABERNATHY, ADAMS, AKERS, ALT, ANDREWS, APPLE/APPELL, ARNOLDS, ATHY, ATKINSON, AYERS, BABCOCK, BACHTEL, BAINES, BARKER, BARNES, BEACHY, BEALL, BEAVER, BECKMAN, BEEBE, BEEMAN, BENNETT, BIBBY, BIDDLE, BIGGS, BISHOP, BLIZZARD, BLUE, BOWDEN, BOWMAN, BRENNEMAN, BROADWATER, BROWNING, BRYAN, BUCHOLTZ, BUCY, BURKEY, CHAPMAN, CHENEY, CHRISTOPHER, CLARK, COFFEY, COMBS, COMPTON, CONNOR, CORBUS, CRAFT, CRESAP, CREUTZBURG, CRITES, CROFT, CROSS, CROWE, CUNNINGHAM, CURRENCE, CUSTER, DAVIS, DAWSON, DAYTON, DEAN, DENT, DICKEN, DOLAN, DONALDSON, DOUGLAS, DURST, DYE, EASTER, EDENHART, EISENTROUT, ELBIN, EMERICK, ERSKINE, ESHLEMAN, EVERLINE, FAKE, FAZENBAKER, FLEMING, FLETCHER, FOLEY, FOOR, FORTNEY, FULK, FULLER, GARLAND, GARLITZ, GEARY, GEATZ, GILL, GILMORE, GOOD, GOODGE, GRANT, GRAY, GREAVES, GRIERS, GRISWOLD, GROVES, GURLEY, HAMILL, HAMILTON, HAMMER, HARPER, HARRIS, HARVEY, HAST, HENDRICKSON, HENRY, HERPICH, HERSCH, HESSER, HICKLE, HIETTS, HILLEGASS, HOLT, HOOPER, HOTT, HOUSE, HUFF, HUMBERTSON, HUTCHINSON, IIAMS, JACKSON, JACOBS, JENKINS, JINKINS, JOHNSON, NEEDHAM, NEFF, NEHRING, NEWELL, NORTH, NORTHCRAFT, NORTON, OATES, ODELL, OFTEN, O'NEAL, ORR, PARKE, PAXTON, PEEBLES, PETERS, PHARES, PORTER, POTTER, PRICE, PRITCHARD, PYNE, RANNELLS, RAVENSCROFT, RICE, RICHARDS, RICHARDSON, RIZER, ROBERTS, ROBESON,

ROBEY, ROBINETTE, ROHMAN, ROLAND, ROSS, RYAN,
SASS, SAVAGE, SAYLOR, SCHARTIGER, SCHMIDT,
SCHRAMM, SCHRIEVER, SCHROCK, SCRUGGS, SEAVER,
SEIFARTH, SHADE, SHAFFER, SHANHOLTZER, SHARPLESS,
SHAW, SHEPPARD, SHIPLEY, SHOBE, SIGLER, SIMPSON   ,
SISLER, SLAGLE, SMITH, SMOUSE, SPEIR, SPENCER,
SPICER, SPRING, STAGGS, STANTON, STEWART, STONER,
STORER, STRATFORD, STREET, STRUCKMAN, SULTZER,
TEMPLE, TETER, THOMAS, THORPE, TRENTON, TRENUM,
TRESSLER, TREZISE, TRIMBLE, TROUTMAN, TRULY,
TWIGG, VANMETER, WAGNER, WAGONER, WAGUS,
WALLS, WARNICK , WAXLER, WEATHERHOLT, WEISER,
WELLS, WENNER, WERNER, WESTFALL, WHALEY,
WHEELER, WHETSTONE, WHITE, WHITTINGTON,
WILHELM, WILLIAMS, WILLISON, WILSON, WILT,
WINTERS   , WITMER, WITT, WOLFE, WOTRING,
WRIGHTSMAN, YOUNGBLOOD, ZIMMERMAN

About the Author

Gary L. Morris worked from 2009 to 2014 as a professional researcher for a major player in the genealogy field. After tracing his family lineage back to 1683, he found that genealogy could be an expensive undertaking. As such, has decided to publish these helpful guides to share the valuable free information he has discovered during his career to help others trace their family lineages as inexpensively as possible. An avid genealogist himself, he hopes you will find this guide factual, thorough, helpful, and most of all, effective in helping you to find your family members.

Notes

Notes